The lives and work of 12 further education based teacher educators in England

Editors:
Roy Fisher and David Powell

Published by University of Huddersfield Press

University of Huddersfield Press
The University of Huddersfield
Queensgate
Huddersfield HD1 3DH
Email enquiries university.press@hud.ac.uk

First published 2023

A CIP catalogue record for this book is available from the British Library.

ISBN Print: 978-1-86218-220-2
ISBN eBook: 978-1-86218-221-9

The editors would like to thank the Education and Training Consortium for its support with this publication.

Contents

Preface

David Powell

This publication was inspired by the work of two Dutch teacher educators: Peter Lorist, of HU University of Applied Sciences Utrecht, and Anja Swennen, of Vrije Universiteit Amsterdam, who have done so much to promote our understanding of the lives and work of teacher educators. To date, they have produced three themed booklets on teacher educators preparing pre-service and in-service trainee teachers to work in primary, secondary and further/adult education. The first of these, a Dutch language publication (Lorist and Swennen, 2015), celebrated the lives of Dutch teacher educators, whilst the second (Lorist and Swennen, 2016) and third, which was guest edited by Liz White (2017), adopted international perspectives. What is clear from this series is the diversity of teacher educators as individuals as well as of the trajectories of their careers and the nature of their work, though there is a common thread: the shadows and impacts of the policy context and of policy makers on these teacher educators' practices, professional identities and on their professional lives. Whilst this booklet is not part of the series produced by Peter and Anja, it adopts the same format: that is one where teacher educators present their stories of becoming and being teacher educators, which appear together with an accompanying account of the policy context in which their work is enacted. As such, it might be seen as a cousin. What is distinctive about this booklet, however, is that it exclusively focuses on one type of teacher educator working in one country: further education based teacher educators in England. The publication of this text was somewhat delayed by circumstances arising from the COVID-19 pandemic. However, this afforded the opportunity for the editors to refer to Loo's (2020) illuminating monograph on the professional development of teacher educators in further education.

Introduction

Roy Fisher

Prosopography, broadly speaking the study of collective biography, is a term which still sends me to a spellchecker - but the field has much to recommend it, and the accounts collected here suggest its potential. Another area of research endeavour which has received more attention in recent years is the study of teachers' memories. What follows, however, is not a presentation of a substantive research project (though it may well provide a 'point of departure' for future studies).

The individual profiles herein will show some of the constituent parts that make up a large network of lifelong learning teacher educators who are, or who have been, based in further education colleges in England. 'Constitution parts' is a cold phrase, and what this booklet aims to do, in a modest way, is to partially illuminate the *people* involved in this work, and aspects of their orientations to being a teacher educator, through a series of relatively short narratives. It is not being claimed that these colleagues are 'typical', of course, each person is unique. What comes through is that collectively, as might be expected, they reflect the (rightly renowned) diversity of the sector which they have been serving.

The life trajectories set out in these accounts range from those of teacher educators who themselves first entered further education as a 'second educational chance', or as part of a journey to a second or a third career, to those of others who arrived through a more direct post-university route. All, however, share a commitment to social justice and to learning or, more specifically, to social justice *through* learning.

There is the road to a career in further education teaching, and then there is the more twisted and less trodden byway that leads to becoming a teacher educator within the sector. What is clear is that the process of becoming never really ends. Common themes, as is the case in a number of other professions, are the pressures that lead to something of an 'imposture syndrome' and, more positively, the strength that is derived from belonging to and actively creating a very real community of practice. The professional and academic synergies and the positive creativity that arise from the these, together with an ethos of genuine partnership, underpin the University of Huddersfield led network which operates through the Education and Training Consortium. This, I think, is evident in these pages.

I hope that you will enjoy reading these teacher educator 'short stories' as much as I did.

Further education based teacher educators, teacher education, and the policy context

David Powell

Teachers of teachers...are typically overlooked in studies of teacher education. (Lanier and Little, 1986, p.528)

A 'normative definition' of a teacher educator might be 'someone who prepares young adults to teach in primary and secondary schools' (Dennis, Ballans, Bowie, Humphries and Stones, 2016, p.9). Unlike those preparing future teachers for primary and secondary schools, further education (FE) based teacher educators in England are working with those who wish to teach, or who currently are teaching, within what is broadly known as the 'Further Education and Skills Sector'. Who are these teacher educators? How do they become teacher educators? Where do they work and what is the nature of that work? What is the policy context? As will be apparent from their stories which follow, policy influences their work and the development of their various identities as teacher educators (Swennen and Volman, 2018).

The English further education and skills sector has been variously known as further education, post-compulsory education and training, and the learning and skills sector; it has been described as an 'important but invisible sector' (Hodgson, Bailey and Lucas, 2015, p.1). It has traditionally been responsible for non-advanced post-compulsory education in England and has a reputation for giving students, 16–18-year-olds and adults, a 'second chance' (Orr, 2016, p.20). However, it has often been seen by politicians 'as the sector for the education of other people's children' (Avis, 2017, p.196). It provides this 'second chance' education and training for about four million students (National Audit Office, 2015, para. 1.1, p.12) and, in 2015, had a budget in the region of £7 billion (p.5). The FE and Skills sector, at its broadest, comprises a number of different types of provider including general further education colleges; specialist further education colleges, such as land-based colleges; sixth form colleges; prisons and young offender institutions; independent training providers; adult and community learning; and voluntary sector organisations. This study, of course, is focussed on general FE colleges. Crawley (2016, p.2) describes the 'working environment [for further education based teacher educators] as particularly diverse, complex, dynamic and challenging'.

Following Murray and Male (2005), FE based teacher educators can be described as second order practitioners in a first order setting, that is, their first order practitioner work was/is as a teacher of their original vocational or academic subject within the FE setting, so their work as teacher educator is 'second order'. Their teacher education work is in a first order setting because it is undertaken in a further education college, rather than in a university (which would be regarded as a second order setting for such work). This is why the teaching professionals featured in this booklet are designated as further education based teacher educators, though some of them may have 'dual identities' in that they may continue to teach their 'first subject' or they may undertake quality assurance or management roles within their colleges (Robinson and Skrbic, 2016). Whatever their identities, there has been, comparatively, something of a 'scholarly silence' in relation to their work (Dennis et al., 2016, p.9). Noel (2006) wrote about the 'secret lives' of further education based teacher educators, and Thurston (2010) described them as the 'invisible teacher educators' because relatively little was known about them, their work and their professional lives.

Loo (2020, p.49) helpfully suggests three 'journeys/pathways to becoming' an FE based teacher educator: 'unintended, intended and miscellaneous.' Those who find themselves on the unintended pathway initially had no intention to become a teacher educator. However, they become a teacher educator after being approached informally by a colleague to join the teacher education team. This informal approach by a colleague was also identified by Noel (2006). The intended pathway is pursued by those who have been inspired by a teacher educator who taught them, and they search out the role as part of their career plan. The miscellaneous pathway, Loo explains, has two routes. The first is 'the cart before the horse' (ibid, p.48), where the person becomes a teacher educator before they become a teacher. This is a route that is rarely taken, I would argue. The second route is 'reluctance, refusal and intentional' (ibid, p.49). This is characterised by the person initially turning down an informal offer from a colleague to teach on a teacher education programme. However, after a period of time, the person accepts the offer and enthusiastically embraces the role of teacher educator. It might be argued that this latter route could easily fit within Loo's 'unintended' pathway.

Work by Noel (2006), Simmons and Thompson (2007), Harkin, Cuff, and Rees (2008), Crawley (2014), Eliahoo (2014), Springbett (2015), and Loo (2020) has contributed to what is known about further education based teacher educators, though it is worth bearing in mind that 11 of the 33 participants in Loo's (ibid, pp. 20-28) study were working in higher education institutions, not FE colleges, according to their 'details'. Noel (2006, p.163) identified that FE based teacher educators were then mostly 'older', white, females; that some of them had not been interviewed for their roles as teacher educators; and that there had at that time been some 'instances of inappropriate recruitment and selection practice, unlikely to promote equality and diversity in teacher educator teams.' Loo's (2020) more recent research reaffirms Noel's findings regarding gender balance and ethnicity. Loo provides data regarding where 32 of the 33 participants in his study were born, their first language and other languages spoken, and their qualifications. Reflecting Noel's earlier work, 26 (81% of Loo's participants were born in the UK, the others having been born in France, Jamaica, Latvia, Malaysia, Poland, and Tanzania.' (Loo, 2020, p.30). 28 (88%) of the participants identified English as their first language, the other first languages indicated were Cantonese, Guajarati, Latvian and French. Other languages spoken included 'French, German, Spanish, Russian, Arabic, Bahasa Malaysia[n], British Deaf Blind, Hausa, Hungarian, Jamaican Patois, Kiswahili, Latin, Mandarin, Polish, Portuguese, Swedish, Urdu and Yoruba…' (Loo, 2020, pp30-31). 27 (84%) had a first degree and 25 (78%) held master's level degrees. Most universities require FE based staff to hold a master's degree in order to be approved to deliver their teacher education programmes. Two participants (6%) possessed a doctorate and four (21%) were working towards a PhD or EdD. Interestingly, 11 (34%) of the 32 did not possess a recognised level 5 or above teaching qualification, though Loo points out that these individuals had degrees or postgraduate degrees in Education.

Simmons and Thompson (2007) observed that the professional lives of further education based teacher educators were significantly different to the lives of those who were university based. They reported that teaching workloads in FE were heavier. FE teacher educators had less 'professional autonomy', they received significantly lower rates of pay, had limited agency in relation to the curriculum they delivered, had fewer 'opportunities for scholarly activity', and they were 'grappling with the problems imposed by limited resources…and an increasingly mechanistic, performatively focused model of teacher education' (Simmons and Thompson, 2007, p.530).

Harkin et al.'s (2008) study usefully analysed the initial or original subject specialist backgrounds from which 88 teacher educators had been drawn. This is presented in Table 1 on page 8.

Subject Specialism	**No. of respondents**
Skills for Life (literacy)	23
Business, management, law & finance	18
English literature & language	8
Health and social care	5
Science	5
Travel, tourism, sport, leisure & hospitality	5
ICT	4
Sociology	4
Psychology	3
Art & design	2
Beauty/complementary therapies & hairdressing	2
Motor vehicle engineering	2
Skills for Life (numeracy)	2
Advice & guidance	1
Agriculture & horticulture	1
Food studies	1
History	1
Special needs	1

Table 1: Teacher educators' subject specialisms (n = 88) (Adapted from Harkin et al., 2008, p.19)

Noel (2006) also identified the original/initial subject specialisms of the teacher educators in her study, though she did not quantify them. Instead, she stated they were:

> …concentrated in certain subject areas – particularly Business & Management Studies and Social Science and Humanities. Their representation in some subject specialisms far exceeds that of the trainees…This is particularly so in relation to ICT, which involves 5% of the teacher educators, 12% of the trainees, and is the subject area with the most learners in FE. Data analysis reveals that over half the centres involve teaching teams with more than one teacher with the same subject specialism, even where the specialism is one not very well represented overall. There are examples of teams with as many as five members from the same background. This evidence of the clustering of specific groupings of teacher educators might suggest that, in some cases at least, a word of mouth, informal type of recruitment is occurring in connection with membership of teacher educator teams. (Noel, 2006, pp.159-160)

Another factor might be the position of 'Education' as a curriculum 'subject' or, more properly, an academic discipline, in its own right within the social sciences. What was particularly useful about Noel's analysis was that it highlighted the clustering of teacher educators around certain subject specialisms and the potential mismatch between them and their trainees' subject specialisms. Powell (2016, p.37) asserted that this mismatch had 'potential implications for modelling and congruent teaching' and teacher educators' ability to enact the subject specialist pedagogies of their trainees within teacher education (Powell and Swennen, 2019).

Drawing on other research relating to transitions in education, Murray and Male (2005, p.127) asserted that the transition from (school) teacher to university based teacher educator was completed within three years. Based on this claim, Boyd, Harris, and Murray (2011) have suggested that inductions for new FE and HE based teacher educators should be undertaken over a period of up to three years; their proposed induction programme would be one that 'deliberately goes beyond the initial year…and includes time to establish identities and roles' (p.7). This might be contested. Another way of looking at this might be to consider the early career years as a teacher educator as an informal period of enculturation (as with most other academic fields). Academics do not normally get 'inducted' into their field in any mechanistic sense. Institutional and departmental inductions are, of course, a different thing (and are most necessary). Perhaps a difficulty with the word 'induction' in this context arises because it implies compliance with known ways of doing things. Views may depend on whether a teacher educator is conceived as some kind of practitioner who acquires a pre-determined skill set or is rather envisaged as an academic (who engages with and, through research and scholarly activity, contributes to an evolving discipline). They may be seen as a form of hybrid. However, it appears that further education based teacher educators may not even receive an induction into their specific role. Following her own empirical study Eliahoo (2014, p.221) observed that '…nearly half of the survey participants had not experienced any induction to the teacher educator role…'. Those inductions which had taken place sat on a 'continuum of quality… from unsatisfactory to conscientious…' (p.130). See also Van Velzen, Van der Klink, Swennen and Yaffe (2010) who have written about the induction of beginning teacher educators. Loo (2020) does not discuss his participants' inductions.

Crawley (2016, p.1) notes that 'within the world of teacher education...[further education based teacher educators] often have the lowest visibility of all.'. For instance, at the 2015 English Universities Council for the Education of Teachers (UCET) Annual Conference there were 9 papers presented on further education based teacher education out of a total of 52; 6 out of 56 papers at the 2016 conference, and 4 out of 44 papers in 2017. There were 4 out of 87 papers at the 2017 English Teacher Education Advancement Network (TEAN) conference. These numbers are low, though they need to be considered in light of the relative size of two sectors: schools and FE&S.

Crawley (ibid) adds that further education based teacher education and its teacher educators are 'rarely mentioned' in policy documents and/or by policy makers. Eliahoo (2014, p.224) asserted that further education based teacher educators might be seen as 'the real victims of benign neglect (Lucas, 2004b, p.35)' within teacher education. However, these teacher educators are responsible for developing the sector's new teachers and trainers and a significant proportion of this work is undertaken in partnership with universities. There are broadly three types of FE initial teacher education (ITE) provision: further education colleges and private training providers offering awarding body qualifications such as the Level 5 Diploma in Education and Training; FE colleges delivering 'franchised' university validated programmes such as the Level 5 Certificate in Education, Level 6 Professional Graduate Certificate in Education, and Level 7 Postgraduate Certificate in Education; and the latter awards delivered directly by universities through their own staff on their own campuses. More rarely a Level 7 Postgraduate Diploma is offered, usually but not exclusively within universities. The teacher educators featured in this booklet are drawn from those who teach at partner colleges within a consortium partnership between more than 20 further education colleges and the University of Huddersfield; it is currently the largest partnership of its type in England. However, the nature of where they work shapes their practice and it is useful to consider the nature of the work they do in comparison with that of university based teacher educators delivering the same or similar provision.

Lunenberg, Dengerink and Korthagen (2014) used data drawn from over 130 journal articles to review and categorise the work of university based teacher educators and classified it into six key roles: teacher of teachers; researcher; coach; curriculum developer; gatekeeper; broker. Drawing on this work and his own research into further education based teacher educators, Powell (2016) identified six primary roles and seven possible additional roles for the FE based teacher educators. These are presented in Table 2 on page 13.

	Primary roles
1	Teacher of teachers, this may be part-time or full-time
2	Gatekeeper
3	Coach
4	Curriculum developer
5	Broker
6	Administrator
	Additional roles
1	Researcher
2	Curriculum manager
3	Staff developer
4	Advanced practitioner
5	Teaching & learning coach
6	Subject teacher
7	Quality assurance

Table 2: Roles of further education based teacher educators (Adapted from Powell, 2016, p.43)

Something is known of the likely job specifications of further education based teacher educators, and the nature of their work, though how many individuals are employed in this role is unclear. Crawley and Eliahoo have estimated 1,500 (Crawley, 2014, p.53) and 2,426 (Eliahoo, 2014, p.51) respectively. However, there has never been a national survey of these teacher educators to establish their number and their professional learning needs, though it has been suggested to the Education and Training Foundation (ETF), an employer-facing, quasi-autonomous national government organisation, that one needs to be done if the work of these teacher educators is to understood and effectively supported.

The English Further Education and Skills Sector has been seen as 'indispensable' by successive governments which have regarded it as a vehicle for implementing their business and skills policies and creating a more skilled workforce (Orr, 2016, p.22); Avis (2017, p.196) described it as 'the handmaiden of industry'. As such, its 'teacher educators play a key role…' (Machin, 2016, p.32) in supporting these aims by providing initial teacher education for new teachers and trainers, many of whom are enacting the government's skills policies in the classroom by training, for example, electricians, plumbers, hospitality staff, health and social care staff, and agricultural workers. Coffield (2015, p.13) asserted that the sector had experienced 'more than 30 years of policy hyperactivity' devised by an ever-changing total of (then) 61 Secretaries of State from successive governments (Orr, 2016, p.19). For instance, Coffield (2008), drawing on research undertaken by Gemma Moss, stated that 459 documents had been sent by 'government agencies to all primary schools in England on the topic of literacy during the years 1996 and 2004…which amounts to 51 per year or almost one a week for nine years' (p.8). Whilst FE teacher education has not suffered the same intensity of governmental activity the lack of political stability that has pervaded education (Orr, 2016) has meant the teacher educators in the sector have experienced 'a permanent revolution' (Coffield, 2008, p.9) that has created an ever accelerating 'pace of change' (ibid.).

Orr and Simmons (2010, p.78), commentating on 'the permanent revolution' (Coffield, 2008, p.8) of educational reform that the FE and Skills sector has experienced, noted that 'virtually all aspects of FE are now highly mediated by the State'. Keep (2006) argues that the FE and Skills sector is now the most highly-regulated and centrally-directed education system in Europe.' This led Hodgson et al. (2015, p.8) to remark that 'England is increasingly an outlier' when compared with other European countries' VET systems as a result of successive governments' neoliberal policies "tinkering and tailoring" (Jephcote and Abbot, 2005, p.181) with the Sector; a process Keep (2006, p.47) described as the educational equivalent of playing with the 'biggest train set in the world'.

The 2007 legislative requirement that all teachers and trainers working in the FE and Skills Sector in England should possess at least a Level 5 initial teacher education (ITE) qualification led to a period of expansion as further education and higher education responded to this policy directive. This framework remained in place until the publication of the Lingfield Report of October 2012 (Department for Business, Innovation and Skills, 2012), which argued that the requirement to have a Level 5 ITE qualification had little impact on the quality of teaching by newly qualified teachers. The subsequent 'de-regulation' of ITE for the Further Education and Skills sector coincided with the introduction of the 'new fees' and student loans, seeing FE ITE fees for some part-time courses increase from c£900 per annum in October 2011 to c£3,000 per annum in September 2012. Many employers were no longer able to, or were not prepared to, pay the fees for in-service trainees and would-be trainee teachers generally needed to apply for student loans. However, the 'de-regulation' did not remove the requirement that all ITE providers are inspected by Ofsted (the Office for Standards in Education, Children's Services and Skills). Awarding body provision within a college is inspected currently as part of the college's inspection, whereas the inspection of provision franchised from a university and delivered by partner further education colleges is inspected currently as part of a university's inspection. In recent years, the 'triple-whammy' of 'de-regulation', higher fees and student loans has seen a number of universities withdraw from further education ITE as the demand for teacher education courses has declined. Tummons (2020, p.17) asserts that 'within this complex and shifting landscape, it is important to acknowledge …FE teacher training continues to rest on a curriculum that remains relatively resilient.' He adds (ibid) that any changes to the curriculum 'reflect changing discourses of what it means to be a teacher, most notably in the coverage of counselling and guidance, and in the provision of study skills.' On page 17, Table 3 presents numbers on enrolments on FEITE courses between 2010 and 2015.

	Type of qualification					
Year	Award	Certificate	Diploma, CertEd & PGCE	Learning & Development Award	Other	Total
2010-11	5,287	3,862**	22,730***	2,937	6,671	41,487
2011-12	36,750	8,600	16,170	Not reported	Not reported	61,520
2012-13	38,730	7,870	12,220	Not reported	Not reported	58,820
2013-14	34,340	6,250	11,450	Not reported	Not reported	52,040
2014-15	25,970	2,920	11,690	Not reported	Not reported	40,580
2015-16	24,170	3,470	10,760	Not reported	Not reported	38,400

Table 3: The number of FEITE enrolments by year and type of qualification between 2010-2015*
(Powell, 2016, p.31; Education and Training Foundation, 2018[1])

The future of further education ITE seems uncertain. Successive governments have continued to intervene in this 'de-regulated' landscape; the latest development being the introduction of apprenticeships in relation to ITE for the FE and Skills Sector in the form of a set of 'Trailblazer' Standards at levels 3, 4, and 5. To what extent these will be adopted remains to be seen. It is within the context that further education based teacher educators work. What follows are some of their stories which provide insights into their often 'hidden' professional lives, academic work, and career trajectories.

1 There have been no reports on FEITE enrolments from the Education and Training Foundation since April 2018

Profiles of 12 further education based teacher educators

John Aston: teacher educator – who would have believed it?

East Riding College, East Yorkshire.

The majority of my working life has been intertwined with education and real evidence of transformational learning of one sort or another. I left school at fifteen (1969) and entered the world of work as an apprentice motor vehicle (MV) engineer. My working week was a combination of work and attendance at Barnsley Technical College. My technical education set the scene for a successful working life as a MV technician, welder, foreman, teacher and, finally, as a teacher educator.

Let me be frank – I was working long hours and was not particularly well paid as a MV technician, so I thought I would have a go at being a teacher and enjoy the long holidays and better pay.

'How hard can it be?' I asked myself. My first port of call was the then Huddersfield Polytechnic (now the University) and an interview for their pre-service Certificate in Education (FE) at their Holly Bank campus. I was accepted and all I had to do was to give up my job and become a full-time student. I did it but what a leap of faith it was when I look back.

In September 1988 I started the CertEd and once things had settled down, I knew teaching was for me. I loved studying and saw the relevance of putting the theory into practice. If I can look for an analogy, I would say it is akin to music playing in my head, the enjoyment and fulfilment of enjoying doing what I do. And to this day that music plays even stronger in my role as a teacher educator. **My role as a teacher educator is a selfless role**, it is not about me, but rather it is about my trainees, many of whom have taken the same leap of faith as I did, who look at me and think: 'give me a good lesson!', 'Give me the pedagogical skills and knowledge to be able to teach properly'. And that is my ethos, simple as that. I have travelled the same road as my trainees and appreciate their anxieties, which allows me to steady their nerves so that they continue with their teaching career with growing confidence.

I loved everything about my time on the CertEd course and, on reflection, it was real evidence of a transformational learning experience if ever there was one. It changed my life and has given me an exciting and interesting career. Education offered me a third chance. It was while I was in my classes at Holly Bank that I knew I wanted to be a teacher educator. Mike Cook, Malcolm Hepworth and David Neve, then teacher educators at the Polytechnic, still influence my teaching and learning strategies to this day.

In July 1989 I gained a full-time position at Scarborough Technical College (as it was then). I quickly settled down into learning how to deliver worthwhile and meaningful lessons. As the years went by, I must have been doing something right as I was asked if I would like to become part of the teacher training team at Yorkshire Coast College (YCC), as it is now called. "Of course", was my reply, "and thanks." So that is how it all started. I worked with Jonathan Tummons, who was also new to the role of teacher educator, so we were as 'green' as each other. However, we complemented each other and developed a team work approach which was probably the best thing for both of us. We were supported mainly by the University of Huddersfield. We also settled into a self-supporting system that was really a community of practice that gave me the real presence and feel of being a teacher educator. I completed a BA (Hons) Education and Training (1998), and then enrolled on the MEd (2005) with the University of Huddersfield. I became Centre Manager at YCC and in 2006 I moved to East Riding College as Curriculum Leader in Education and Teacher Training, where I worked in partnership with Jane Chadwick without whom the centre would not be thriving as it is today.

My role as a teacher educator has been such a privilege where I still have that same belief in education as a transformative experience as when I first started at Holly Bank in 1988. What a story and what a journey I have had, and I would not change a thing. But what is important to me is this question: have I made a difference? If I have, then it is in very large measure down to the University of Huddersfield and the real transformational learning I experienced both on my CertEd and subsequent development by the team at the University.

Postscript *Since John wrote his profile, he has retired as a full-time teacher at East Riding College and now works as a teacher educator at the University of Huddersfield on a part-time basis.*

Gail Bailey: being a teacher educator

Nelson and Colne College, Lancashire.

I first thought about being a teacher as far back as when I was at primary school, but as I started secondary school (and became a slightly rebellious teenager) I decided against university after completing my A levels. However, I did gain a Higher National Diploma (HND) and my career choice led to me having my own small, successful business for the next 23 years. I have no regrets; my experience of self-employment has been an advantage throughout my working life. My background was massage and beauty therapy and, alongside running my business, in 1998 in Clitheroe, Lancashire, I began to teach in Beauty Therapy and Massage and did this for approximately 12 years before taking up a full-time teaching position in 2010. I did my PGCE in 2002 via a distance learning programme offered at the time by University of Greenwich – this suited my then circumstances and I am grateful for it.

Throughout my early teaching career, I taught from Entry Level up to Level 4 and my part-time lecturing gradually became much more important to me than my business, so it was somewhat fortuitous when a full-time position became available. I loved teaching and I was good at it; inspiring the next generation and watching them develop, make progress and achieve was what drove me, but I still needed more of a challenge.

In 2011 I began a BA (Hons) in Education and Professional Development with Huddersfield University, and the new knowledge and confidence I was gaining led to me applying for, and being appointed as, an Improvement Practitioner role in 2012, where the main focus was on supporting teaching, learning and assessment across our organisation. I combined this role with my other teaching work and now I was regularly delivering professional development sessions to colleagues. Whilst this was terrifying at first I found that, together with my degree studies, I was building up a portfolio of new pedagogical skills, and I was enjoying my new journey immensely. Mid-way through my degree it became clear to me that I wanted to now teach people how to teach and this became my main focus. I had had significant success in my degree with my first year tutor awarding my presentation on lesson observations and the function of Ofsted 95%, the highest mark she had ever given, and this served to inspire me further to develop my own practice and that of others. This tutor, Rebecca Clare, was passionate about education and a fount of knowledge; I felt very privileged to have been taught by her and she certainly motivated me to want to do even more.

The opportunity to begin to teach on the teacher education programme was offered to me during a regular meeting with my line manager, who was the head of Initial Teacher Education at the time. I had never mentioned wanting to teach on the programme but instead **it was suggested to me as my next step**. This encouraged me even further as I had been recognised as having the skills needed to develop the next generation of teachers in the sector.

As my degree came to a close another position of Teaching Excellence Hub Manager became available and I applied for it as this would be perfect alongside my new role as a teacher educator, which would begin in September 2014. Thankfully I was successful and although I had a big learning curve ahead of me it was a challenge I was ready to take on. There was much to learn as I was teaching a new subject, at a higher level, along with a new management role. On reflection, it was a lot to take on all at once but I was determined and relished the opportunity to carry on learning.

To deliver the modules I was re-engaging with pedagogical theories and feeling more able to analyse these and critique them in ways I had felt less inclined to do in my early teaching years. Both then and now I question whether we can teach someone how to teach, or is it an innate skill akin to the art of being a good communicator? Are we are simply equipping natural teachers with the tools and strategies they need to teach successfully in line with what government agenda deems the best way? **I want new teachers to see that I am still excited and motivated to learn**. The desire to go on learning is of the greatest importance, according to Dewey, and nowhere can this be more important than in teacher education.

Postscript *Since Gail wrote her profile, she has left Nelson and Colne College and is Head of Teaching and Learning at Myerscough College, near Preston.*

Sally Brown: an unlikely teacher educator

Wakefield College, West Yorkshire

My parents were told categorically that I would never be able to contemplate a career which involved standing up and talking in front of anyone, I was painfully shy at school, and **the last thing I imagined was that I would become a teacher**. As such I chose to become a psychiatric nurse and, once qualified, had a variety of different roles within the NHS supporting people with mental illness. It was only as I started to mentor student nurses on placement that I experienced the joy of facilitating learning, and, in 1993 I embarked on my first teaching qualification through City and Guilds; the Further and Adult Education Teachers' Certificate. I was confident in my own subject knowledge, but not in my ability to teach. My confidence grew, and when my daughter started attending the local pre-school, I was asked to help out on the parent rota. I subsequently joined the Committee and helped secure funding for a course designed to equip new parents to consider a career in childcare. The only problem was that there was no tutor for the course, and as the only one with a teaching qualification, I soon found myself working as a sessional tutor and subsequently a Regional Training Officer, a full-time post with the Pre-school Learning Alliance. One of my responsibilities was to recruit new tutors, and as the sector changed in response to the introduction of the 2007 regulations, I found myself undertaking an in-service Postgraduate Certificate in Education at Wakefield College.

Linda Hallwood was my tutor, and the Centre Manager at Wakefield. I found her to be inspirational and motivating, she was passionate about the role of an FE teacher, and at my final tutorial asked me what I hoped to do at the end of the course. My answer was 'I would love your job, and to inspire other teachers in the same way you inspired me!' The introduction of the 2007 standards caused a surge in recruitment of new teachers to the sector and when, subsequently, some temporary hours became available within the teacher education team at Wakefield Linda encouraged me to apply. A month after starting this work I was offered a full-time post, and a year later Linda chose to reduce her hours. I applied for the Centre Manager post and succeeded her in 2009, a post I still hold today.

I am passionate about the pivotal role that teachers within the sector play. Despite my then shyness I had thoroughly enjoyed my time at school and I have studied almost continually ever since. However, this is not always the case for those accessing education and the support of a good teacher can have a significant impact in terms of engaging and inspiring adult learners. This was emphasised when one of my learners, who would go on to successfully complete a Level 3 teaching qualification, was so nervous before his micro-teach to the rest of his peers that he was physically ill. Notwithstanding this he went on to secure volunteer teaching hours in September the same year and embarked on the in-service Certificate in Education. Throughout his two years on the course, he grew both in terms of confidence and academic ability, and by the end of the second year, not only had he justifiably been given an outstanding grade across all four areas but had secured a paid teaching position in a further education college. He graduated at the age of 55 having left school with no qualifications and having been told by his teachers that he would 'never amount to anything'.

I completed my doctoral research in 2018; my thesis was entitled 'What does professionalism mean to teachers within further education?' This study seeks to understand the concept of professionalism in relation to trainee teachers currently undertaking initial teacher training within further education. This was prompted by the de-regulation of ITE across the sector following on from the Lingfield Report in 2012, which, coupled with the significant increase in tuition fees, has seen a decline in the number of trainees. A key driver in my choice of research topic and interest stemmed very much from the following quote from Robson (2006) 'The assumption has been…that if I know my subject, I can, by definition, teach it to others'. That certainly was not my experience when I started teaching student nurses, undertaking ITE equipped me with the skills and knowledge to teach others, and I am heartened that, despite the ever-changing landscape in further education, there are still many who are committed to professionalism and ITE.

Brenda Campbell: becoming a teacher educator

The Manchester College

I left school in 1979 to become a secretary and embarked upon a number of courses that included shorthand, typing and administration training. I worked in this role from 1987 until 1993 before being made redundant. In 1995, I returned to education, as I wanted to improve my English and maths, in particular maths as I had left school without this. Furthermore, I wanted to undertake a Psychology course in the hope of becoming a counsellor. Teaching was the furthest thing from my mind at that point.

I chose an access course and excelled in both the course work and exams. I did particularly well in maths and found myself helping some of the other learners who were struggling. My then English teacher, Lorna Roberts, asked me if I had thought about going to university.

Her belief and unwavering support that I could do this helped me make the decision to apply for three different university courses and I finally chose to study a BA in Applied Human Communication because it was psychology-based. I successfully completed this in 1998 and over the following summer I became restless and knew that I would like to progress further but was unsure about the area I wanted to pursue. I spoke to Joe Whittaker, a lecturer at the University of Bolton, and decided to apply for the pre-service PGCE and to teach English as my subject specialism.

Once qualified, my first teaching post was at a local community centre where I taught 16-18 year olds life skills, including English and Maths, in order to prepare them for either further education, training or employment. A significant moment was when I saw the learners, all of whom had been previously excluded from school and felt that they could not turn their lives around, successfully complete, and either get jobs or progress to other courses. I continued this work until 2002 as I felt I needed to move onto a larger organisation to reach a wider cohort which included teachers. I then joined The Prince's Trust, a charity working with unemployed young people, as a teacher with responsibility for embedding English and maths into community programmes for 16-25 year olds. Alongside this, I also successfully completed my level 4 literacy subject specialist certificate. In 2005, I was again made redundant. A vacancy became available within the Teacher Education department at MANCAT, subsequently renamed The Manchester College following a merger, where I have remained to date. Moving into teacher education was a key moment in my career. It has seen me teach a number of initial teacher education awards from level 3 to level 7, as well as being given the responsibility for delivering CPD for colleagues across the College. This has been both challenging and rewarding.

A number of people have inspired me on my journey to becoming a teacher educator. Joe Whittaker, who taught me on the PGCE, was a strong advocate for inclusive learning. I gained an immense wealth of knowledge from him that I would go on to apply to my teaching years after qualifying. **Creativity is an important element of my teaching and I ensure that this is embedded in each lesson that I deliver, modelling effective practice**. The Teacher Education team at The Manchester College, along with two members that have now left, Libby Mooney and Dr. Titilola Olukoga, have inspired my creative teaching. As a team we share ideas and plan lessons together to ensure that our trainees have the best experience. Modelling our practice ensures that lessons are fun and engaging as well as delivered to a high standard.

I have gained in-depth knowledge of teacher education through academic critical friendships, scholarly activity and informal discussions regarding teaching and learning, which enabled me to gain the confidence to move forward to complete my MA in Education. This developed my research skills and directed my interest in the areas of autoethnography and Critical Race Theory. I hope to progress further by completing a doctorate.

Adam Hewitt: from punching numbers to pedagogy

The Manchester College

I have always been incredibly indecisive and when I was young I had many career aspirations, including author, teacher, and marketing manager, but I was very undecided until I reached my mid-twenties. When I left university I was still unclear on a career path. I wanted to teach but knew I did not want to work in the primary or secondary sector, so after completing an undergraduate degree in English Language and Linguistics at Sheffield University I trained to be a management accountant instead.

With forty years of endless spreadsheets looming I heard by chance in 2004 about a course at Bolton Institute of Higher Education (now the University of Bolton) to become a literacy subject specialist and train to teach in further education, a sector with which I was unfamiliar, so I gave up my career and studied a one-year full-time programme. It was this journey with Bolton that led me in to being a teacher and teacher educator, and **I knew on the first day of my teacher training that my ultimate goal was to be a teacher educator** because I felt very connected to the content and was keen to support new teachers in the way I was being supported.

By 2009 I was managing a curriculum area at Hopwood Hall College in Rochdale when Gill Waugh, my former tutor, and Head of Initial Teacher Education at the University of Bolton, asked if I would like to deliver a continuous professional development module on behalf of the University. I jumped at the chance and taught there one evening a week on top of my full-time role at the College. Later that year a member of staff at the University of Bolton was going on maternity leave and I successfully applied for their job, which I took on secondment for twelve months. Twelve months lead to two years, and then to some part-time work with the University and various other universities around teacher education and English, and these opportunities were significant in my journey towards working full-time in teacher education.

Two people stand out as being influential in my journey to where I am today. Gill Waugh gave me my initial opportunity to work in teacher education and it is unlikely I would be where I am today without this chance. I still see elements of her teaching in my teaching and I learnt some valuable lessons from her about what it means to be a teacher educator. Ela Owen was my manager when I worked in a college in Oxfordshire, and she showed me that teacher education should be much more than a script or an assignment, as well as the importance of reflection and conversations with trainee teachers to bring out the best in their practice.

In my first few years as a teacher educator I felt very reliant on other people to support my development. It was a very steep learning curve and I would spend hours looking at other people's materials to ensure that I understood them and that I could deliver them with confidence. I felt like I was treading water a lot of the time but reflecting on the experience now it has made me more resilient when delivering courses in what is a fast changing and developing environment.

As my career has developed I have become much more interested in and focused on doing my own research and preparation for sessions and on ensuring that I am working towards supporting trainees to be great teachers, not just to meet criteria set out in a handbook. The conversations I have with colleagues in my current role have been invaluable, and **I have found that informal discussions in the staffroom are now where most of my personal learning and development takes place**.

I have always felt too busy to pursue further study (I was going to complete an MA full-time in 2005 but decided against it because of work) but I subsequently enrolled on an MA in Education and I am now working towards achieving this goal. The MA is proving beneficial for both me and my students. For example, it has allowed me to reflect on how students' own lived experiences translate in to their professional practice, and how students can use this to challenge their own ideas about teaching and learning.

Rajiv Khosla: I was meant to lead the retail revolution, not teach.

City of Liverpool College

Becoming a teacher was never one of the career options discussed in my teenage and early adult life either at school by our careers advisors or at home by my parents, neither was it one that I considered myself. I was destined to take over my father's retail business which he had established in 1966, after working in the cotton mills in Manchester after his arrival in England from India in 1961. Predictably this is exactly what I did! After a reasonably satisfactory (disappointing in my parents' eyes and clearly requiring improvement) education, acquiring a HND (with distinction) at Newcastle Polytechnic in Public Law and Business Administration, I turned down the offer of enrolling on Year 2 of a Law degree and decided to make my fortune in the world of retail clothing. It was this journey that ultimately (albeit 12 years later) led me to Bolton Institute to enrol on a full time Certificate in Education course.

January 2001 was the start of this major change in career. My business was declining mainly due to the opening of the Trafford Centre in Manchester (at the time one of largest out of town shopping centres in Europe). Our brands were in direct competition with the likes of Selfridges, and it was becoming increasingly difficult to survive. As the lease was up for renewal in May 2001, I decided to give notice to the landlords of my intention to terminate the lease agreement. Judith, one of my regular customers (and now very close friend), became aware of this and offered me a post within their travel company as an Operations Director on a six months' contract. It was this work with Judith, and her husband, Maurice, that was career changing. Both Judith and Maurice had been teachers and had set up a travel company taking school groups on coach tours to Paris and Disneyland Paris. It was the work with these school groups that planted the seed to become a teacher. In September 2001 I had enrolled on a full time Certificate in Education course with a government bursary of £6000 (how times have changed) as there was a national shortage of teachers.

One of the most significant moments in my teaching career was during a family visit to Slovakia during Easter 2002. I was invited to 'meet' an English teacher at the local grammar school by my wife's aunty. I ended up teaching English to 10-18 year olds for a week - something surely was lost in translation? I was 'observed' by my wife at every lesson as she was acting as my interpreter. My first post was a Schools and Careers Liaison Officer for the work-based learning provider I did my teaching practice with in Horwich, Bolton. I soon obtained a full-time role within Alliance Learning teaching Basic Skills Maths and progressed to managing the Skills for Life provision and a small team of English and Maths tutors. During this time I also successfully obtained a Level 4 teaching qualification in teaching Maths and volunteered as a mentor at Bolton Lads and Girls Club. However, my management role resulted in endless meetings, reports, data analysis and this meant I was only teaching 1 or 2 hours per week, and I decided I needed a change. I had come into teaching for a change in career and I was desperately missing the interaction with students in the classroom. I applied for and was successful in gaining a post at Liverpool Community College in 2006 as a lecturer within the Teacher Education team. **I have been fortunate to work with many inspirational and influential colleagues** during my time in Liverpool, but the most notable was Maire Daley, who was my mentor when I joined the team and when I was appointed as an Advanced Lecturer. Maire's drive, enthusiasm, passion, and intelligence was incredible. I learnt so much from working with Maire and this has provided me with many of the skills and qualities that I possess as a teacher today. My former manager, Mick Smith, was also a great inspiration and his support and encouragement led me to complete a MA in Advanced Educational Practice and complete training as an Additional Inspector for Ofsted.

Since becoming a teacher educator, there have been many changes both at a macro and micro level. The increased scrutiny and use of performance management surveillance systems has unfortunately driven many experienced teachers out of FE and led to the decline of potentially new teachers entering the sector. In these challenging times, I feel it is important that teachers in the sector retain the intrinsic feeling of empowerment in order to maintain their drive, enthusiasm, and passion for teaching and for their own personal well-being. Controlling my own personal CPD, retaining my personal values and ethics, and maintaining my interests and hobbies outside of work have enabled me to continue to develop into the teacher educator that I am today.

Postscript *Rajiv left City of Liverpool College and worked as a teacher educator at Riverside College, Widnes until September 2020. In October 2021, he began re-training to become a tax inspector.*

Heather Lister: the accidental teacher educator

Selby College, North Yorkshire

My parents always said that I was a 'born teacher'. Apparently as a child, I would try to teach my dolls things. Nevertheless, I was adamant I did not want to be a traditional teacher who went to school, then to university and straight back to school. As I had always loved languages and communicating with people, I completed a BA (Hons) in Modern Languages and also studied Business at Université Laval, Quebec, Canada. I then worked for ten years in export sales and marketing in the textile industry. In 1990, prior to the creation of the European Single Market, I decided to make a career change and started to teach Business French and German, and thoroughly enjoyed seeing my students progress. Soon afterwards I got a job teaching Modern Languages and Business Studies at Selby College. I taught a wide range of age groups and levels from Adult Education to 16-18 year olds, BTEC Level 1 to 'A' Levels and so I enrolled on an in-service PGCE with the University of Huddersfield to deepen my understanding of teaching, learning and assessment and to hone my teaching skills.

Like many teacher educators in further education, **my entry into teacher education was very much by chance**. Although my subject specialisms were Modern Languages and Business Studies, I was asked one day if I would be interested in teaching a City and Guilds (C&G) 7307 Stage 1 Introduction to Teaching evening class. I was given a course overview, books by Geoff Petty and by Reece and Walker, and shown the filing cabinet with some resources in. I enjoyed the challenge and 'got by' with a little bit of help from a colleague/mentor who answered a few of my questions, but I was not really guided in how to train future teachers.

I subsequently taught on C&G 7307 Stage 2 and then in 1999 I was asked to join the Certificate of Education/Postgraduate Certificate of Education (Cert Ed/PGCE) team. **I questioned whether I had the subject knowledge, skills, and experience to be a teacher educator** and to teach at higher education (HE) level, but my then line manager assured me that as I was a good teacher, I would be a good teacher educator.

Fortunately, the then Cert Ed/PGCE course leader, Glenys Richardson, pointed me in the right direction in terms of content to be delivered and interpretation of assessment criteria, and helped me assess work, but I did feel rather a fraud. How could I train teachers when I sometimes had bad teaching sessions myself? So, I read more books and discussed teaching and learning issues with colleagues in the hope of gaining some enlightenment in relation to the art of teaching.

My approach to teacher education was pragmatic: I encouraged trainees to discuss their lessons and reflect on their practice. Inspired by a course in 'advanced practice and creativity' led by John Beverley, formerly of Huddersfield Technical College, I endeavoured to give trainees practical ideas for activities and a toolkit of skills which they could use in their lessons. It was only later when I did a course at the University of Huddersfield on developing evidence-based teacher education practice, led by Penny Noel, that I was to learn that this approach was called 'modelling'.

In fact, it was not until I became Centre Manager and regularly attended University of Huddersfield meetings, conferences and undertook a MA in Education and Training that I really began to consider in any depth the nature of teacher education and to critically engage with the literature.

Another key person in my development as a teacher educator has been my colleague, Jane Brooke. Together we have not only shared ideas and good practice but have also undertaken research projects into ways to support our sometimes 'fragile learners'. Furthermore, our experiences of teaching trainees working in offender learning, together with colleague Ellen Schofield, were also influential in my developing a broader understanding of teaching in what was known as the 'post-compulsory sector'.

Throughout my career I have continued to teach 'A' Level French and German because I think that teaching specific subjects gave me credibility with our trainee teachers. As I have become increasingly aware that teaching is not an exact science or an art, but a juggling act, requiring the insights of a psychologist and the virtuosity of a jazz player. I still often feel a fraud trying to train teachers to face the challenges of the classroom as well as the demands of their senior managers and of Ofsted.

John Matthews: it was a long haul to teacher educator

Hull College (retired)

Developing into a teacher educator seems to have been a theme for most of my working life. It all started in industry in my early twenties. Having completed a recognised apprenticeship in mechanical engineering in 1968, I progressed to being a draughtsman at a company that made glass containers in Doncaster. It was here that I got my first experience of speaking to groups about the role of engineering design and its contribution to the production processes. This was quite a daunting task for a 23-year old but I enjoyed it. Therefore, when an opportunity presented itself to go into training full-time I did not need to think too hard about it and I became an Instructional Officer in what was then called a 'Government Training Centre'.

During my early years as a trainer I also managed to secure part-time teaching jobs in what was then Hull College of Higher Education and at the then Hull Technical College. Moving to a full-time appointment in a college was at that stage an ambition but I did not have the necessary qualifications for a full-time post. This all changed when in the early eighties the then Conservative Government, concerned by the rising numbers of unemployed school leavers, introduced The Youth Training scheme (YTS). To be involved in this new area of work colleges changed their academic requirements for lecturing staff and I was successful in securing a post at Hull College of Further Education. I like to think that my reputation as a part-time teacher was also an influencing factor. The College required me to complete 'The City and Guilds Further and Adult Education Teachers Certificate' course and this gave me my first insight into teacher education as well as giving me the ambition to become a teacher educator. The first two years of lecturing were tough. The students were mostly unmotivated and in this difficult context my part-time Certificate in Education course at Huddersfield Polytechnic did little to inspire me or raise my spirits.

Probably the greatest influence in becoming a teacher educator was when a colleague, who I had a lot of respect for, and who was influential in the College, suggested I seek some work with the adult training team. Thus, I joined a team of four lecturers who were expected to deliver teaching and training skills, mainly to people in industry who were involved in the increasing number of YTS courses. This move was a breath of fresh air. I was constantly being told that I was good at it and better than that I was enjoying it. There were two other significant events over the next few years. First in 1988, I took my first steps into teacher education when The City and Guilds 7307 was transferred from what was then Hull College of Higher Education to the teacher education team at Hull College. Second, in 1993 the Hull College entered a franchise agreement to deliver the University of Huddersfield's Certificate in Education and PGCE.

I was appointed to the position of Centre Manager for the Huddersfield provision because of my role in setting it up at the College and, as most of the students embarking on Cert Ed/PGCE were College staff, **it quickly dawned on me how high profile I had become within the College**. Staff attending the courses had high expectations of the teacher educators and any criticisms would flow in my direction. There were two things which I feel were important to us as the teacher education team established its reputation. First, the curriculum model recognised and placed great value on meeting the particular development needs of each trainee. Second, through my 13 years as Centre Manager I worked with very talented and dedicated teacher educators who were role models for the trainees. Both were important when, in 2001, the then Labour Government introduced a requirement for all FE teachers and trainers to have at least a level 5 teaching qualification (this requirement would be removed by the Coalition Government in 2013). Labour's initiative meant that in 2001 staff who had been teaching in colleges for many years, but had not yet gained a teaching qualification, had to enrol on the CertEd or PGCE – and some, it must be acknowledged, did this with a measure of reluctance.

I have now been retired over 10 years, but I maintain an interest in teacher education and I regularly meet with former colleagues who keep me up-to-date. The end of the requirement for teachers and trainers to have at least a level 5 teaching qualification seems to be a short-sighted approach, probably influenced more by cost cutting than anything else. During my time as a teacher educator I saw standards rise as more people enhanced their teaching skills and knowledge through the courses they attended. **Hopefully, the policy makers will once again recognise the fundamental importance of teacher education** and its role in preparing and developing the sector's most valuable asset.

Lou Mycroft: a principled teacher educator

Northern College, Barnsley

I never did decide to become a teacher educator and it was not until I read Lunenberg, Korthagen and Swennen's work on modelling that I realised the meta-function of what I did.

I was a public health specialist in a pioneering NHS department, which promoted community development as the most effective vehicle for empowerment (and consequently health improvement) – this was my master's study and remains my professional heartland. I joined Northern College to work on a Community Health Animateur programme; a practical expression of my public health work. I did not identify as a teacher at that time, never mind a teacher educator, yet in essence the work I did then is the work I do now.

For twenty years, I have worked with people who, whether they identify it or not (generally not), have a leadership role amongst marginalised groups and individuals. Teacher education, rather than community regeneration or public health, is now the approach I take but I have come to be pragmatic about the labels disciplines carry. Language mutates but the mission is still social change.

Three key moments in my development were:

1. Joining the Consortium Network and its community of practice.
2. Realising that I could lead the co-creation of new pedagogies and theories of learning.
3. Foregrounding the principle of equality in the TeachNorthern 'Community of Praxis'

Along the way, I have been inspired by:

- Cheryl Reynolds, Jebar Ahmed and Alison Iredale, all of whom are digital pioneers.
- Shailesh Appukuttan and Catina Barrett, who inspired me to think of myself as a thinker.
- Liz O'Brien, one of Northern College's trainees, for her tweet which sparked the idea of the TeachNorthern Community of Praxis and 'thinkers are our friends', the notion that writers are not to be feared but befriended as they help us map out and better understand our roles as teachers and trainers and the places where we practice.

The biggest shift in my thinking has been from teaching content to process. At the start of my career as a teacher educator I worked hard to learn about other people's pedagogies, to transmit this information to trainees in a number of active and 'busy' ways. Now I combine digital and face-to-face stimuli with dialogic pedagogical processes, which enable students to think critically and deeply, identifying their own pedagogies, theories of learning and leadership strategies and putting them into practice.

And I have come full circle. From health to education, community development's *yin* - and the corresponding *yang* of organisational development - have been at the heart of my own praxis. A further shift this summer has provided a life-changing perspective. 'The work' (the political work of shifting the world's inequalities) is the institution, rather than any single institution being 'the work'. Whether I am writing, teaching, teacher educating, researching, campaigning, reading, tweeting or just out in the world meeting people, **I am doing my bit to change the world.**

Postscript: *Lou has completed her doctorate since writing her profile.*

Kim Sanderson: becoming a teacher educator

Harrogate College

My journey to being a teacher educator was not intentional; it evolved as a result of twenty years' experience of teaching and managing a range of curricula in a further education college.

I did not even have aspirations to become a teacher until my late twenties, despite spending a year as a teaching assistant in a French secondary school as part of my undergraduate degree. It happened after I had been working in a management role for a large well-known retailer. I was responsible for running staff development sessions; a standard weekly 30 minutes of top-down dissemination of information from Head Office to staff. I knew there was something lacking in this method of staff training, although at that time I could not articulate what it was. I just knew that to really improve the quality of customer service and increase sales; the staff needed to be more involved in the process. I could either pay lip service to this or I could do it properly. Thus, I started to create short activities to get staff to talk more about what we were doing. I loved it and wanted to do more of this kind of staff development. I chose the post-16 education sector because I wanted to enhance people's employment skills and my degree in French and Spanish was my starting point for application onto a full time PGCE in 1993. In the early days of my career, I travelled to further education colleges in North Cheshire, York, Bradford and to Harrogate College, where I taught a mixture of French, Spanish, and retail business subjects. This later led to leadership and management roles at Harrogate College in a variety of curriculum areas including business and languages.

In 2009, I was invited to be a mentor for a PGCE student and this was the initial introduction to working as a teacher educator. I really enjoyed working with new teachers and supporting them through the early days of their careers. I loved the enthusiasm that they brought with them. In 2010, I started teaching PTLLS, a level 3 ITE award, and carried out observations of CertEd and PGCE students. I felt supported by fellow teacher educators in my staff room as we discussed standardisation of assessment and the enhancement of feedback to the trainees. These conversations were invaluable to me as a new teacher educator.

Despite this support, I experienced the often reported 'imposter syndrome' and reckoned it was probably just a matter of time before I would I be 'found out'. Enrolment onto a master's level study could only enhance my credibility; short CPD updates no longer had sufficient validity if I was going to take this role seriously. As part of the master's study in Professional Development, I became very interested in a teacher's sense of agency and this inspired me in my work with trainee teachers. Over the last 20 years or so, I have experienced many government funding cuts and my own specialist subject area (languages) disappeared entirely from the offer in my own college. It is easy to feel powerless in these circumstances and I knew that being open to change was crucial for survival if I wanted to stay in the sector. Even though an individual teacher has relatively little control over government policy decisions, they do have control over what happens in their classroom. How a teacher deals with their own students and organises learning activities is totally within their remit. This is an area that I like to discuss with trainee teachers if they express feelings of constraint and negativity towards an aspect of their work. In an ever-changing landscape of government policy and funding drivers, two key attributes for survival are resilience and flexibility.

An interest in developing people is a key reason for being a teacher educator. For me, this has only been possible with opportunities for continuous professional development and supportive colleagues and managers who are interested in developing tutors so that their skills are deployed effectively. **I am proud to continue this culture of learning with trainee teachers** and other newer colleagues who are starting on their journey. Returning to my initial reasons for moving into teaching from a retail background, I think the reasons are the same, that is, we are on a quest to continually improve quality and we can only do this through a shared venture and by offering support to tutors from the earliest stage of their careers.

Postscript: *Since Kim wrote this profile, she has left and is currently at Leeds Beckett University.*

Corrine Scandling: from 2 'O' levels to a master's degree

Kirklees College, Huddersfield

I left school at 16 with no real idea of what I wanted to do. I had not enjoyed the last 2 years of my schooling, missing classes and not engaging with my teachers but I did manage to leave with 2 GCE 'O' levels and mediocre Certificates in Secondary Education (CSEs) [these awards were, together, the predecessors of GCSEs]. This was sufficient to get me a job as a junior clerk/secretary in a local engineering company and I was required to attend my local college one day and one evening a week. This I did enjoy and engaged with. It was the start of my lifelong learning journey. For the next three years I undertook and successfully passed relevant qualifications in secretarial studies and then, at the age of 23, realising I no longer wanted to be a secretary, mainly due to the fact that I did not feel challenged enough and felt capable of doing more, I moved into youth training to teach/train what was known as office skills. This new job allowed me to teach the skills I had acquired to those who wanted to be secretaries.

My journey into becoming a teacher educator began in 2000 at what was then Huddersfield Technical College (HTC), now Kirklees College. I was teaching part-time at Her Majesty's Prison and Young Offender Institution (YOI) New Hall as well as at HTC teaching key skills. I was asked to join a small team at HTC to develop and then deliver the City and Guilds (C&G) 7307 to a cohort of trainee teachers specialising in childcare and early years. This council-led initiative was a response to the investment in early years education by the then Labour Government and aimed to meet the expected demand for more childcare and early years teachers by training childcare and early years practitioners. Although not a practitioner, I had been chair of a pre-school governing body and of an after-school club.

Initially I was quite intimidated by teaching trainee teachers in a field I was not an 'expert' in, however, I quickly realised that it was not about teaching them their subject knowledge, they had this, it was about teaching them to teach, and I could draw on my own experience of teaching in different environments to different types of learners. My experience of teaching different subjects at the prison/YOI had taught me that if you identified a theme for teaching a specific subject on one course, this could often be adapted and be taught on others. This is something I still draw on today when my trainee teachers are struggling with how to embed English and maths into their lessons.

In 2001 I decided to move into a full-time teaching role at HTC, which would allow me to continue teaching on the C&G 7307. The main factor in my decision to move to the College was I had got a thirst for learning and wanted to do something more substantial rather than focusing on short courses, so I opted to undertake a BA (Hons) in Education and Training with the University of Huddersfield. This was a course I was more than ready for, and I fully utilised the relevant modules to develop my own academic ability but also as a means to improve my teaching. As I came towards the end of the degree things began to change very quickly in initial teacher education and the expectation that new teachers would require a Level 5 teaching qualification created an opportunity to teach the University of Huddersfield's CertEd and Professional Graduate Certificate in Education at my college. I was initially quite overwhelmed teaching on these courses, especially year 2, but the support within my college and through the monthly network meetings at the University were invaluable in helping me through this transition.

In 2008, recognising how important it is to keep up-to-date with what is going on in the sector, I started a master's degree and completed this in 2011. As a teacher educator, **what motivates and inspires me is to get my trainee teachers engaged and aware of issues that are impacting on them and their teaching practice.** I actively encourage the use of digital technologies within my lessons and keep up-to-date myself, there is so much out there but **I learn from the trainee teachers as well as them learning from me.** I am a huge advocate of promoting dual professionalism and how important it is to be at the forefront of developments in teaching and learning as well as what is happening within government and policy.

Rachel Terry: still becoming a teacher educator

Calderdale College, Halifax

In one sense, I became a teacher educator in 2006 when I gained a role within the teacher education team at my college, delivering sessions on the Minimum Core to Cert Ed/PGCE cohorts and training support tutors in literacy skills. My past experience as a modern linguist and ESOL teacher probably got me the job. In another sense, however, **I am still becoming a teacher educator**, aware that it is not a clearly marked transition, but a journey plagued by feelings of impostership and doubt.

The first lesson I taught on the Cert Ed/PGCE ended in a round of applause, perhaps triggered by the trainees' recognition that I had just pulled off a significant survival feat. I felt intensely aware of my lack of theoretical knowledge, my own PGCE in secondary education having taught me approaches to teaching languages, without touching on many of the theorists that dominate other teacher education curricula. I could almost feel these theorists hovering disapprovingly at my back. From regarding myself broadly as an effective ESOL teacher, I now felt as if I was a beginner again, using session plans that had been created by my predecessor and struggling to find my own voice.

A key turning point was a *Train the Trainers* course for literacy and ESOL teacher educators (or trainers) in 2009. Here I was able to engage with theory as a living element of practice, as well as filling in some gaps under the pretext of 'revision'. We considered explicitly the characteristics of teacher educators as opposed to teachers, the first time that I had been encouraged to recognise the difference. Teacher educators were marked by the need to be 'emotionally robust', strong enough to subject their own practice to scrutiny by themselves and others, and, indeed, to use this as a teaching resource. Somehow this helped me to appreciate that it would never be easy but that my own learning as a teacher was potentially more valuable than my (still lacking) 'expert' knowledge. As I went on to teach a BA Education for the first time and then to start my own EdD, **reading and learning became a part of my everyday practice**, I was also subtly influenced by each of the other members of the teacher education team at Calderdale College, learning from the different ways in which they carried out the role and interacted with students. By the time Debs Philip left the College in February 2014, I felt equipped to step into her shoes as Centre Manager, even if I made the shape and style of those shoes very much my own.

But a deeper sense of fraudulence still lurks somewhere beneath. Becoming a 'teacher educator' implies that you once became a teacher, in my case, immediately after my degree, unsure what to do with my life and feeling that a PGCE would at least appear purposeful. Although I successfully passed the course, I was not yet emotionally equipped to deal with the school environment and, after a short spell of fairly disastrous supply teaching, opted out. When I opted back in in 2002, this time teaching ESOL in an FE college, I was surprised to find that I could teach and that I could even deem myself a 'good' teacher. I now realise how loaded a term this is, drawn back repeatedly to Moore's (2004) excellent study of 'dominant discourses' in teaching and teacher education. Rather than essentialising the properties of a 'good' teacher (or teacher educator) he advocates the 'reflexive turn', which offers 'the best hope, however uncomfortable [...] of long-term professional happiness and improvement of classroom practice' (p.141). I have since introduced this to my trainees, to encourage them to recognise that good teachers come in many different forms and are unlikely ever to be the 'finished product'.

The same applies, of course, to me as a teacher educator. The journey continues, but it is now slightly more comfortable and significantly more self-aware.

Postscript: *Since Rachel wrote this profile, she has left Calderdale College and joined the University of Huddersfield as a senior lecturer in teacher education. In addition, she has successfully completed her doctorate.*

Drawing some conclusions: 8 key themes

David Powell

Livingston (2014, p.219) recognised that the role of teacher educator is no longer solely university based and called for 'a better understanding' of teacher educators 'working in different locations and educational sectors'. This booklet can be seen as a modest response to Livingston's request, one which should be seen as part of a wider mosaic of emerging work in this area. There is no claim that these further education based teacher educators are necessarily representative of others working in the sector, though the telling of their stories may contribute to the mapping of further education based teacher educators and their work (Petrie, 2015). Thematic analysis (Braun and Clarke, 2006) of these 12 stories offers eight insights into the lives and work of these further education based teacher educators which are outlined below.

1. Academic background

Unlike those teacher educators involved in the training of school teachers, for the majority of these FE based teacher educators the route into teaching was generally not the traditional academic path of GCE A Levels followed by a university degree before moving on directly to a full-time teacher training course. Five of them, however, had followed that route. The other seven had undertaken vocational and professional qualifications in areas such as engineering, beauty therapy, secretarial studies, and nursing before entering some form of teacher training after a career within their respective occupational fields. This reflects the vocational nature of the further education curriculum, though perhaps not so strongly as might have been imagined. This may be a consequence of a persistence of some of the subject specialist issues referred to by Noel (2006), as well as the strongly social scientific nature of Education as a discipline.

2. Triple professionals

Given the vocational nature of FE it is, perhaps, unsurprising that 10 of the 12 started their employment careers outside teaching. Teachers in further education in England who first enter teaching in this way have sometimes been characterised as 'dual professionals' (Robson, 1998, p.603): their first profession being their career before teaching; the second being teaching. For instance, John Aston was a motor vehicle technician, welder, and foreman before he taught; Sally Brown and Lou Mycroft worked in England's National Health Service. Their moves into the role of further education based teacher educator is then their third professional identity. The regular incidence of this kind of professional profile led Crawley (2014, p.121) to describe further education based teacher educators as 'triple or multiple professionals'.

3. Roads to becoming a teacher

Three of the teacher educators mention having had an early ambition, or their parents having had an ambition, for them to teach from early in their lives - Adam, Gail, and Heather – though they did not enter teaching immediately. Adam trained to be a management accountant:

> With forty years of endless spreadsheets looming I heard by chance in 2004 about a course at Bolton Institute of Higher Education (now the University of Bolton) to become a literacy subject specialist and train to teach in further education, a sector with which I was unfamiliar, so I gave up my career and studied a one-year full-time programme.

Gail reflected: 'I first thought about being a teacher as far back as when I was at primary school', though it was sometime later, after running her own business, that she moved into teaching, initially on a part-time basis. Rachel tells us she was 'unsure what to do with my life and feeling that a PGCE [Schools] would at least appear purposeful.' However, she reflexively discusses how she 'was not yet emotionally equipped to deal with the school environment and, after a short spell of fairly disastrous supply teaching, opted out.' She would return to teaching later.

For the majority of these teacher educators teaching was a relatively late career choice, and the move to becoming a teacher educator was frequently one which was determined by an element of 'happenstance' (as indicated below).

4. Being identified as a potential teacher educator by another teacher educator

> ...one becomes a teacher educator by being a good teacher... (Russell and Korthagen, 1995, p.190).

Seven of these teacher educators' stories indicate that they were invited to join the teacher education team by an established teacher educator within their college. In that respect, the transition was not initiated by a proactive choice on their part. As such, this is what Loo (2020, p.48) calls an unintended pathway to becoming a teacher educator. This 'making of an unsolicited approach' by a senior teacher educator seems to have been an established practice in the recruitment of future further education based teacher educators (Noel, 2006). For instance, John Matthews reflected: 'Probably the greatest influence in becoming a teacher educator was when a colleague, who I had a lot of respect for and who himself was influential in the college, suggested I seek some work with the adult training team.' Corrine had a similar experience: 'I was asked to join a small team at HTC [her college] to develop and deliver the City and Guilds (C&G) 7307 to a cohort of trainee teachers specialising in childcare and early years.' Kim's journey started with a request for her to be a mentor:

> I was invited to be a mentor for a PGCE student and this was the initial introduction to working as a teacher educator...In 2010, I started teaching PTLLS, a level 3 ITE award [at that time], and carried out observations of CertEd and PGCE students.

5. Being inspired to become a teacher educator by another teacher educator

For five of these teacher educators the teacher educators who taught them as they were doing their own initial teacher education provided the motivation for them to become teacher educators themselves. Loo (2020, p.49) calls this an 'intended pathway' to becoming a teacher educator. Sally identified Linda Hallwood, a teacher educator at Wakefield College as 'inspirational', adding: 'she was passionate about the role of an FE teacher, and at my final tutorial asked me what I hoped to do at the end of the course. My answer was I would love your job, and to inspire other teachers in the same way you inspired me!' Gail singles out Rebecca Clare as her inspiration: 'She was passionate about education and a font of knowledge; I felt very privileged to have been taught by her and she certainly motivated me…', though it would take a suggestion from her line manager that teacher education might be her 'next step' for that to happen.

The factor underlines the importance of the long-established notion that teachers provide role models (see 7. below).

6. Undertaking educational research

Lunenberg et al. (2014) identifies researcher as one of the roles of the teacher educator. Maintaining current knowledge of academic debates and emerging knowledge is fundamental to effective teacher education. All the teacher educators featured here were active in regularly attending professional development events and contributing to the surrounding scholarly debates, three of these FE based teacher educators had chosen to formalise their research activity by currently undertaking, or had completed, professional doctorates: Sally, Rachel, and Lou.

7. The importance of role modelling, and of peer and team support in the transition into the role of teacher educator

The transition from teacher to teacher educator was not straightforward. New identities were grappled with, and the constantly evolving knowledge requirements of teaching the teacher education curriculum presented some challenges. This can be a solitary and lonely experience for some teacher educators (Ritter, 2011), in which support can be an 'unmet expectation' (Yamin-Ali (2018, p.76). Seven of these teacher educators identified colleagues who had acted as role models and supported them in their new role. For example, Brenda wrote:

> Joe Whittaker, who taught me on the PGCE, was a strong advocate for inclusive learning. I gained an immense wealth of knowledge from him that I would go on to apply to my teaching years after qualifying…The Teacher Education team at The Manchester College, along with two members that have now left, Libby Mooney and Titilola Olukoga, have inspired my creative teaching. As a team we share ideas and plan lessons together to ensure that our trainees have the best experience.

Rajiv identifies the contribution of Maire Daley, who was his mentor, and Mick Smith, his former manager, to his development as a teacher educator:

> Maire's drive, enthusiasm, passion, and intelligence was incredible. I learnt so much from working with Maire and this has provided me with many of the skills and qualities that I possess as a teacher today…Mick…was also a great inspiration and his support and encouragement led me to complete a MA

in Advanced Educational Practice and complete training as an Additional Inspector for Ofsted.

Heather identifies two teacher educators who helped her develop her knowledge and her practice:

> …the then Cert Ed/PGCE course leader, Glenys Richardson, pointed me in the right direction in terms of content to be delivered and interpretation of assessment criteria, and helped me assess work…Another key person in my development [was]…my colleague, Jane Brooke. Together we have not only shared ideas and good practice but have also undertaken research projects into ways to support our often 'fragile learners'.

Interestingly, Heather adds that some of her trainees (student teachers), who worked in prison education, and another colleague, Ellen Schofield, helped her develop and broaden her 'understanding of teaching' in the sector.

Adam names Ela Owen, his former manager, as someone who supported him as he became a teacher educator: 'she showed me that teacher education should be much more than a script or an assignment, as well as the importance of reflection and conversations with trainee teachers to bring out the best in their practice.'

To conclude, Corrine's story provides a reminder of how significant the transition into the role of teacher educators can be and of the key roles that colleagues and a wider network can play in supporting new teacher educators: 'I was initially quite overwhelmed teaching on these courses, especially year 2, but the support within my college and through the monthly network meetings at the University were invaluable in helping me through this transition.'

8. Feelings of vulnerability in the role

> It is only natural that problems related to self-confidence would emerge in interviews with novice teacher educators. It is rather surprising, however, that the experienced teacher educators did not mention this topic at all. (Kremer-Hayon and Zuzovsky, 1995, pp.161-162)

Four of the teacher educators mentioned their feeling anxious or experiencing a sense of impostership at some stage early in their role. Corrine reflected that 'I was quite intimidated by teaching trainee teachers in a field I was not an 'expert' in.' This, however, did not last long for her as she realised that she was teaching her trainees how to teach and how to be a teacher. Rachel feels 'a deeper sense of fraudulence still lurks somewhere beneath. Becoming a teacher educator implies that you once became a teacher' and her story suggests this was far from straight-forward. Rachel employed Moore's (2004, p.141) notion of the 'reflexive turn' to make sense of her previous experiences as a teacher in the 'hope' of finding 'long-term professional happiness'. Kim felt that, in spite of support from colleagues, she 'experienced the often-reported imposter syndrome and reckoned it was probably just a matter of time before I would I be found out.' Whilst Heather's line manager assured her that she was a good teacher, she 'did feel rather a fraud. How could I train teachers when I sometimes had bad teaching sessions myself?', she asked herself.

Kremer-Hayon and Zuzovsky (1995, p.162) suggested that a lack of confidence in a teacher educator could have two possible consequences: it could create feelings of 'frustration' or it could provide a stimulus for professional development as a means to address any feelings of inadequacy.

Far from final thoughts

Roy Fisher and David Powell

The stories told in this booklet underline that there is no typical further education based teacher educator. The teacher educators who contributed come from a range of academic and professional backgrounds, and they followed varying individual routes into teaching, and then into becoming teacher educators. They have indicated something of who they are, yet there is inevitably much more to learn about their work. For instance, it would be interesting to build on Kremer-Hayon and Zuzovsky's (1995) now somewhat distant work on the professional development of teacher educators and to learn more about this in relation to further education based teacher educators. It would be illuminating to study further education based teacher educators' dispositions towards their work as researchers within their field and the broader area of Education Studies.

What we have presented here is a series of brief career related biographies. They each seem to celebrate the identity of 'teacher educator', but they also collectively project a strong sense of liminality which pervades the professional journey taken and which remains palpable even after many years. The role of teacher educator does not really constitute a terminal destination. Like all biographical details these stories take place in a particular context and that context is framed by institutional, sector and professional regulation, it is engrained in complex cultures and very particular personal and occupational histories. FE teacher education, of course, is enacted as a practice in relation to the wider field of school teacher education, which in the UK has its own long established traditions based on full-time residential training in, often, single-sex teacher training establishments of the kind described by Edwards (2001). These school teacher training colleges generally offered a process of bourgeois enculturation, frequently within a religious ethos. It was these roots that contributed to teacher education's relative conservatism as an academic activity (Ellis and McNicholl, 2015), and to a situation in which teacher educators,

> ...were produced as an exceptional category of academic worker in this sense and also in the sense of bearing strong personal responsibilities as professional role models and exemplary practitioners. (Ellis, McNicholl and Pendry 2012 p.691)

John Furlong (2013), focusing on universities, has set out the development of Education as an academic discipline, including the political and policy challenges that have impeded it and those which face it. In some respects, the recognition related challenges described by Furlong become amplified within FE based teacher education, and this is particularly so in relation to the issues which lead to academic marginalisation. For many, the margins are a favoured site of labour, the place where it is most possible to 'make a difference'.

These 12 narratives offer a modest contribution to what is known about further education based teacher educators in England and stand as an invitation to others to tell their own stories as part of their continued contributions to educational discourse.

Appendix

Methodology

David Powell

This study was undertaken in the spirit of prosopography, a methodology sometimes employed by historians. In doing this, they might 'single out relevant factors such as age, social, cultural, and professional backgrounds, that may help to identify underlying social processes and thus discover unexplored features of causation' (Cordillot, 2000, p.234). In this instance, we have drawn on 'narrative and biographical data' from the 12 'career stories' (Kelchtermans, 2009, p.260) of these further education based teacher educators who are currently, or who have been in the past, teaching on the University of Huddersfield's initial teacher education programmes. These teacher educators are/were based within partner colleges of the Education and Training Consortium, an initial teacher education partnership between the University and more than 20 FE colleges, at the time they wrote their story. The idea for the booklet was shared at one of the University and partner colleges' regular 'Network meetings' as a way of recruiting potential participants. Research by Noel (2006) on the Consortium's further education based teacher educators more than a decade earlier had concluded that they were then predominantly female and 'older'. The twelve participants for this study were recruited through a combination of volunteer, snowball, and purposive sampling. We were particularly pleased that Brenda and Rajiv tell their stories because minority ethnic teacher educators are under-represented in the further education based teacher education workforce, though it should be stressed that this was far from the most important reason that their accounts appear here.

Drawing on my experience of writing my personal profile for inclusion in Anja Swennen and Peter Lorist's booklet (2016), I asked each participant to write a 750-word profile of themselves that answered the following questions, all of which were based around those used by Peter and Anja:

- When did you decide (first think about) becoming a teacher? [And…] a teacher educator?
- What were the most significant moments in you becoming a teacher educator?
- Who have been the key people in your journey to becoming and being the teacher educator you are today?
- How did you develop as a teacher educator in those first few years? How have you developed since then?

This approach intentionally used the accessible, everyday language of their practice, what Loo (2020, p.6) calls 'a language of articulation' (Loo, 2020, p.6), to help elicit their experience of becoming and being teacher educators. Once the profile had been written, each storyteller was invited to select one or two quotations from their story that they felt captured the essence of their professional lives and work. Their accounts were then analysed to identify themes, located within the existing literature and from this conclusions were drawn (Wellington, 2000).

References

Acker, S. (1997). Becoming a teacher educator: Voices of women teacher educators in Canadian Faculties of Education. *Teaching and Teacher Education*, 13(1), 6-74.

Avis, J. (2017). Beyond cynicism, comfort radicalism and emancipatory practice: FE teachers: In M. Daley, K. Orr, & J. Petrie (Eds.), *The Principal: Power and Professionalism in FE* (p195-202). London: IOE Press.

Boyd, P., Harris, K., & Murray, J. (2011). *Becoming a Teacher Educator: Guidelines for the induction of newly appointed lecturers in Initial Teacher Education*. (2nd ed.). Bristol: ESCalate.

Braun, V., & Clarke, V. (2006). Using thematic analysis in psychology. *Qualitative Research in Psychology*. Vol 3 (2), pp77-101.

Crawley, J. (2014). *How can a deeper understanding of the professional situation of LLS teacher educators enhance their future support, professional development and working context?* (PhD thesis). Retrieved from https://www.academia.edu/10701131/Crawley_J_2014_How_can_a_deeper_understanding_of_the_professional_situation_of_LLS_teacher_educators_enhance_their_future_support_professional_development_and_working_context

Crawley, J. (2016). Introducing the 'invisible educators'. In J. Crawley (Ed.), *Post compulsory teacher educators: connecting professionals* (pp1-7). St. Albans: Critical Publishing

Coffield, F. (2008, October). When the solution is the problem... *UCU Newsletter*. pp.9-10.

Coffield, F. (2015, March). *Resistance is fertile: the demands the FE sector must make of the next government*. Keynote at New Bubbles Conference, 26 March 2015.

Cordilliot, M. (2000) (French-speaking radicals in the USA: the possible usage of prospography [Biographical Dictionary of French-speaking Radicals in America]. *Labour*. Issue 45. Spring 2000. Page 234. https://www.proquest.com/scholarly-journals/accoun-speaking-radicals-usa-possible-usags/docview/218789920/se-2?accountid=11526

Dennis, C.A., Ballans, J., Bowie, M., Humphries, S., & Stones, S. (2016). Post compulsory teacher educators: the 'even more' quality. In J. Crawley (Ed.), *Post compulsory teacher educators: connecting professionals*. (pp. 8-15). St. Albans: Critical Publishing

Department for Business, Innovation and Skills (DBIS). (2012). *Professionalism in Further Education: Final Report of the Independent Review Panel Established by the Minister of State for Further Education, Skills and Lifelong Learning. The Lingfield Final Report*. London: Department for Business, Innovation and Skills.

Education and Training Foundation (2018). *Initial Teacher Education Provision in FE: Second year report*. London: The Education and Training Foundation.

Edwards, E. (2001). *Women in Teacher Training Colleges, 1900-1960: a culture of femininity*. London: Routledge.

Eliahoo, R. (2014). *The accidental experts: a study of FE teacher educators, their professional development needs and ways of supporting these* (PhD thesis). Retrieved from https://discovery.ucl.ac.uk/id/eprint/10021749/

Ellis, V. & McNicholl, J. (2015). *Transforming Teacher Education: reconfiguring the academic work*. London: Bloomsbury.

Ellis, V., McNicholl, J. & Pendry, A. (2012). Institutional Conceptualisations of Teacher Education as Academic Work in England. *Teaching and Teacher Education*, 28. 685-693.

Furlong, J. (2013). *Education – An Anatomy of a Discipline: rescuing the university project?* London: Routledge.

Harkin, J., Cuff, A., & Rees, S. (2008). *Research into the Developmental Needs of Teacher Educators for Effective Implementation of the New Qualifications for Teachers, Tutors and Trainers in the Lifelong Learning Sector in England* – DRAFT INTERIM REPORT. Coventry: LLUK.

Hodgson, A., Bailey, B., & Lucas, N. (2015). What is FE? In A. Hodgson (Ed.), *The coming of age of FE? Reflections on the past and future role of further education colleges in England* (pp1-24). London: IOE Press.

Jephcote, M., & Abbott, I. (2005). Tinkering and Tailoring: the reform of 14-19 education in England. *Journal of Vocational Education and Training*, 57 (2), 181-202.

Keep, E. (2006). State control of the English education and training system – playing with the biggest train set in the world, *Journal of Vocational Education & Training*, 58 (1), 47-64.

Kelchtermans, G. (2009). Who I am in how I teach is the message: self-understanding, vulnerability and reflection. *Teachers and teaching: Theory and Practice*. 15 (2), 257-272.

Korthagen, F., & Russell, T. (1995). Teachers who teach teachers: Some final considerations. In T. Russell & F. Korthagen, (Eds.), *Teachers who teach teachers: reflections on teacher education* (pp187-192). London RoutledgeFalmer.

Kremer-Hayon, L., & Zuzovsky, R. (1995). Themes, processes and trends in the professional development of teacher educators. In T. Russell & F. Korthagen (Eds.), *Teachers who teach teachers: reflections on teacher education* (pp155-171). London: Routledge Falmer.

Lanier, J. & Little, J. (1986). Research on teacher education. In M. Wittrock (Ed.), *Handbook on research on teaching* (3rd ed.). (pp.527-569). New York: MacMillan Publishing Company.

Loo, S., (2020) *Professional Development of Teacher Educators in Further Education: Pathways, Knowledge, Identities and Vocationalism.* Routledge.

Lorist, P., & Swennen, A. (Eds.). (2015). *Maatschappelijke wortels van lerarenopleidingen.* Utrecht: Hogeschool Utrecht.

Lorist, P., & Swennen, A. (Eds.). (2016). *Life and work of teacher educators*. Utrecht: Hogeschool Utrecht.

Livingston, K. (2014). Teacher educators: hidden professionals? *European Journal of Education*, 49 (2). Retrieved from DOI: 10.1111/ejed.12074

Lunenberg, M., Dengerink, J., & Korthagen, F. (2014). *The Professional Teacher Educator: Roles, Behaviour, and Professional Development of Teacher Educators*. Rotterdam: Sense Publications.

Orr, K. (2016). The filling in the educational sandwich: post compulsory education. In J.Crawley (Ed.), *Post compulsory teacher educators: connecting professionals* (pp16-23). St. Albans: Critical Publishing.

Orr, K., & Simmons, R. (2010). Dual identities: the in-service teacher trainee experience in the English further education sector, *Journal of Vocational Education & Training*, 62 (1), 75-88.

Machin, L. (2016). The history and development of post compulsory teacher education. In J. Crawley (Ed.), *Post compulsory teacher educators: connecting professionals*. (pp24-33). St. Albans: Critical Publishing

Murray, J. & Male, T. (2005). Becoming a teacher educator: evidence from the field. *Teaching and Teacher Education*, 21 (5), 125-142.
Moore, A. (2004). *The good teacher: dominant discourses in teaching and teacher education*. London: Routledge Falmer

National Audit Office (2015). *Overseeing financial sustainability in the further education sector*. London: National Audit Office HC 270 July 2015.

Noel, P. (2006). 'The secret life of the teacher educator: becoming a teacher educator in the learning and skills sector'. *Journal of Vocational Education and Training*, 58 (2) 151-170.

Petrie, J. (2015). Introduction: How Grimm is FE. In M Daley, K. Orr, & J. Petrie (Eds.), *Further education and the twelve dancing princesses.* (pp.1-12). London: IOE/Trentham.

Powell, D. (2016). "*It's not as straightforward as it sounds": an action research study of a team of further education based teacher educators and their use of modelling during a period of de-regulation and austerity (*EdD thesis). Retrieved from http://eprints.hud.ac.uk/id/eprint/32137/

Powell, D. & Swennen, A. (2019). Leren onderwijzen door leren kijken: Een opleidingsdidactische benadering [Learning to teach by looking: A pedagogical approach]. In G. Geerdink & I. Pauw (Eds.), *Opleidingsdidactiek: Hoe leiden we leraren op?* [Pedagogy for teacher educators: How do we educate teachers] (pp. 43-54). Vereniging Lerarenopleiders Nederland. (Kennisbasis katern 7).

Robson, J. (1998). A profession in crisis: status, culture and identity in the further education college. Journal of Vocational Education and Training. 50 (4), 585-607.

Robson, J. (2006). *Teacher Professionalism in Further and Higher Education: Challenges to Culture and Practice.* Abingdon: Routledge

Robinson, D., & Skrbic, N. (2016). Invisibility or connecting professionals. In J. Crawley (Ed.), *Post compulsory teacher educators: connecting professionals* (pp42-49). St. Albans: Critical Publishing.

Ritter, J. (2011). On the Affective Challenges of Developing a Pedagogy of Teacher Education, *Studying Teacher Education*, 7 (3), 219-233.
Russell, T., & Korthagen, F. (1995). Teachers who teach teachers: some final considerations. In T. Russell & F. Korthagen (Eds.), *Teachers who teach teachers: reflections on teacher education* (pp187-192). London: Routledge Falmer

Simmons, R. & Thompson, R. (2007). Teacher educators in post-compulsory education: gender, discourse and power, *Journal of Vocational Education & Training*, 59 (4). 517-533.

Springbett, O. (2015). *Enacting professional identity: An exploration of teacher educators' entanglement with educational technologies in FE* (PhD thesis). Retrieved from https://eprints.lancs.ac.uk/id/eprint/76235/

Swennen, A. & Powell, D. (2020). Brave Research as a means to transform teacher education. In A. Swennen & E. White (Eds.), *Being a Teacher Educator: Research-Informed Methods for Improving Practice.* (pp155-170). London: Routledge

Swennen, A. & Volman, M. (2018). The development of the identity of teacher educators in the changing context of teacher education in the Netherlands. In J. Murray, A. Swennen & C. Kosnik (Eds.), *Inside teacher education: International perspectives on policy and practice* (pp. 107-121). Springer.

Thurston, D. (2010). The invisible educators: exploring the development of Teacher Educators in the Further Education system. *Teaching In Lifelong Learning: A Journal To Inform And Improve Practice*, 2 (1), 47-55.

Tummons, J. (2020). Teaching the new professionals: a recent history of teacher education and teacher professionalism in the further education sector in England. In S.Loo. *Professional Development of Teacher Educators in Further Education: Pathways, Knowledge, Identities and Vocationalism* (pp10-18). London: Routledge.

Wellington, J. (2000). *Educational Research: Contemporary Issues and Practical Approaches*. London: Continuum.

White, E. (Ed.) (2017). *Teacher educators' pathways to become research active.* Utrecht: Hogeschool Utrecht.

Van Velzen, C., Van der Klink, M., Swennen, A., & Yaffe, E. (2010). The induction and the needs of beginning teacher educators. *Professional Development in Education*, 36 (1-2), 61-75.

Yamin-Ali, J. (2018). Tensions in the work context of teacher educators in a School of Teacher Education in Trinidad and Tobago. *European Journal of Teacher Education*. 41 (1), 66-86.

Roy Fisher
Email: r.fisher@hud.ac.uk

Roy is Emeritus Professor of Education at the University of Huddersfield where he was, prior to his recent retirement, Head of the Department of Initial Teacher Education. He began his teaching career in further education, where he first made the transition to working as a teacher educator. He was founding chair, then co-chair, of the Yorkshire and Humberside Learning and Skills Research Network from 1998 to 2008. Roy was, until 2018, a long-standing member of Management Forum of the *Universities Council for the Education of Teachers*. He was for many years a member of the editorial board of the *Journal of Vocational Education and Training*. His work has been widely published and has encompassed, inter alia, teacher education, subject specialist pedagogy, vocationalism, the history of education, and representations of education in popular culture. He is a Principal Fellow of the Higher Education Academy.

David Powell
Email: d.powell@hud.ac.uk

David is a Senior Lecturer in Teacher Education at the University of Huddersfield. He started his further education (FE) career at Stafford College in 1986 (his father taught Graphic Design there from 1964-1994). David moved from a senior management role, via staff development, into further education based initial teacher education (ITE) in 2005. In 2009, he joined the University of Huddersfield as a Senior Lecturer in Teacher Education. Between September 2014 and April 2020, David was director of the Education and Training Consortium, an ITE partnership between some 20 FE colleges and the University of Huddersfield and the editor of *Teaching in Lifelong Learning: a journal to inform and improve practice* aimed at the further education sector. His research interests include further education based teacher educators' use of modelling, how student teachers learn how to teach, and 'brave research' (Swennen and Powell, 2020) and brave researchers.

David is a member of the Association of Teacher Educators in Europe (ATEE). Between 2019 and 2022 he was an elected member of its Administrative Council and co-chair of its Professional Development of Teacher Educators' Research and Development Community (RDC). Since October 2020, he has been a governor on the Board of Wakefield College.

Between September 2014 and April 2015, he led an Education and Training Foundation funded project to write a 'How to' guide on embedding the 2014 Professional Standards into initial teacher education (ITE) courses. He has been a member of the Education and Training Foundation's FE ITE Working Party since its inception in May 2015. In March 2016, he led an Education and Training Foundation (ETF) funded project to produce a CPD framework for teachers and trainers working in the Further Education and Skills Sector in England. In January 2019, he was a member of the team awarded a contract by the Welsh Government to undertake a scoping study to inform the development of a professional learning framework for the post-16 learning sector in the principality.